Born in Managua, Nicaragua, Maria-Teresa del Carmen is the author of *A Visitor Awaits You*, a book she will be submitting for publication. She lives in California.

To
my beloved sister, Damaris;
my beloved father, Ramon Felipe-Nery;
my mother, Lidia Amada;
my brother Ramon Felipe;
my aunt, Martha.

Maria-Teresa del Carmen

THE DRAGONFLIES IN MY MIND

AUSTIN MACAULEY PUBLISHERS™

LONDON · CAMBRIDGE · NEW YORK · SHARJAH

Ordering Information
Quantity sales: Special discounts are available on quantity purchases by corporations, associations, and others. For details, contact the publisher at the address below.

Publisher's Cataloging-in-Publication data
del Carmen, Maria-Teresa
The Dragonflies in My Mind

ISBN 9781647500856 (Paperback)
ISBN 9781647500849 (Hardback)
ISBN 9781647500863 (ePub e-book)

Library of Congress Control Number: 2022915084

www.austinmacauley.com/us

First Published 2022
Austin Macauley Publishers LLC
40 Wall Street,33rd Floor, Suite 3302
New York, NY 10005
USA

mail-usa@austinmacauley.com
+1 (646) 5125767

This book could not be published without the support and encouragement I received from my beloved sister, Damaris. She was a person who believed in me and for this I loved her dearly. I want to thank my supervisor, Elena, for believing in me and in my work. I want to give special thanks to, Dr. Linda Woodall, she has been an anchor in my life.

Prolonged Destiny

Managua, Nicaragua. The day was October 29, 1959. It was a quiet afternoon when not a soul was seen on the streets. Managua seemed to have been sleeping as if hiding from the intense humidity and heat. Outside in the hospital's corridor a slim, young man, was pacing and chasing away the **dragonflies.** The slim, young man almost drowned in his own perspiration which he alleviated by smoking one cigarette after the other. His wife was about to give birth to their second child. Waiting for the moment at the hospital, the woman was lying down in the position to give birth and suddenly without any notice, a baby girl left her mother's womb as if she was impatient for the nine months she was inside of her.

The newborn baby girl was destined to live only for a matter of seconds after her birth, if it was not for a lady janitor who was mopping the floor. The lady janitor was able to catch the baby girl in her arms before she would hit the floor and depart from this world, taking with her nothing but a few breaths of the clean smelling air from the recently mopped floor by the unknown woman janitor. Did anyone know or ask who she was? Did anyone ever thank her? Did the woman janitor really exist, or was she an angel?

The woman janitor, a prolonged destiny, the **dragonflies**; a mystery, a moment which was frozen and captured in time as it left a forever expression in the baby girl's face.

I am Maria-Teresa, the newborn baby girl you were just reading about, at the age of 43. I was chosen to be initiated in a lifetime of wondering and questioning; of thinking I had the answers to soon enough ask the same questions. I was chosen to be initiated in a lifetime of feeling intensively; of loving without limitations, the same with suffering. And as a person from Nicaragua, I was chosen to a lifetime of adjusting to the sequels left after earthquakes, war and relocating to the U.S.A., the challenges of coming to terms with my sexual preference. I was also chosen to a lifetime of living and coping to meet the challenges brought with major depression and with the challenges brought with attention deficit hyperactivity disorder ADHD.

My First Weeks of Age

From the hospital, I was taken home, and placed in the loving arms of Theo, our nanny. She was a strong and soft woman in her thirties. A woman who for each of my mother's births would come to the city and would stay with us until the newborn was two to three years old. She would then leave to go back to take care of her own family. Theo lived in a small farm between Managua and Diriamba—a city located North West of Managua.

I was baptized with the name of Maria-Teresa del Carmen. I was named after the woman who together with her husband had raised my mother since the age of three. My biological maternal grandfather was gunned down by the National Guard from Nicaragua and my grandmother remarried. Back in that time it was not accustomed for parents to bring along children from a prior marriage into a new marriage. This was done in the best interest of the children and thus my mother was given away. The couple that raised my mother to me and my siblings were like our real grandparents. We loved them dearly.

As with any other children in the family, during my first weeks of age my parents took me to the ocean. That part of the Pacific Ocean between Masachapa and Pochomil where we co-owned a beach house with other relatives. The wonder of the most serene, yet tempestuous of places was introduced to me at such an early age. It was as if my parents knew that the serenity of the ocean to which I was introduced at an early age, would become some sort of cushion in the preparation for the tempest that would come later in my life. The ocean, that place where happiness and tranquility abounded for to this date in time, the recollections of such place come to my mind bringing that same happiness and tranquility, with only one difference; this time the happiness and tranquility comes accompanied with nostalgia.

My First Recollection

The moment of my first recollection was at about the age of two years old. We were at El Abra, a farm owned by some oldest relatives on my father's side. The house was the typical country house with high colonial ceilings, with the exception of the dining room which was like an annex to the house. The ceiling in the dining room was about seven feet tall. We were having dinner sitting at the dining room table which accommodated at least eight people. My relatives were enjoying a good meal accompanied by a conversation, which ended when I spilled a glass of pinolillo which is a typical Nicaraguan refreshment made of ground toasted corn and cacao beans.

The normal paced moment turned into slow motion as I remember the expressions of people who were at least five times my size. The content in the glass spilled in an area as large as the table itself. I never lost site of the pinolillo as it spread on the table. A quiet moment followed as my mother picked up the mess I had made. A silent moment, for no one expressed a word or emotion. I still wonder why I would recollect that moment.

Of my next early years of age, I have no recollection, only pictures. On these, I can see I brought lots of happiness to those around me, especially to Roger—my oldest brother who was my playmate before my other brother and sisters were born. I brought lots of happiness also to my biological maternal grandmother who became a very close friend of mine.

Tamara

During the year of 1963, my sister Tamara was born. I was playing a game of drawing lines on the sidewalk with two of our neighbors. Our game ended when I saw my father and mother coming back home from the hospital. I felt a great deal of happiness when I saw my mother holding a very slim baby girl with lots of hair on her head and with very long hands. She was so slim and fragile that at such an early age I did not know if Tamara smiled or cried; perhaps she did both at the same time. Our nanny, Theo was back with us on the day Tamara was brought to our house. Sometimes I wonder if in addition to her duties Theo was also paid to give us the love and affection my siblings and I needed. One thing I know is that there were rumors that Theo not only gave love to the children in our home but to my father also.

The years were going by and still my brother and I could not figure out when Tamara laughed or cried. This would get Roger and me in lots of trouble. Tamara would sometimes lie and accuse us of doing bad things to her; and since she would easily cry her heart out, she inspired lots of protection from my mother and father who would blindly believe Tamara's accusations, and Roger and I would get punished if not hit with the 'ramal.' The ramal was a man's leather belt my mother folded and cut into four branches to hit us. My mother used the ramal mostly on Roger, who would never be still.

Kindergarten

The year of 1964 was also very special because it was the year when I started school. Theo was extra nice with me that morning. She sang and talked to me in a loving and very fun way as she bathed and dressed me. The night before my first day of school was very exciting; my mother prepared my uniform and left it ready for me to wear the next morning. Everything I wore that day and during the whole first week of school was brand new. My father drove my mother and I to 'The Immaculate Conception,' an all-girl catholic school located in the heart of Managua, that is the 'old Managua'— which is the name we used to distinguish the capital of Nicaragua before the city was destroyed by the earthquake in 1972.

I was matriculated in a half-time boarding school program and attended The Immaculate Conception School from kindergarten until my first year of High School. The nuns of this school belonged to the congregation of Saint Frances Xavier-Cabrini. Mother Clemencia was my first teacher. She was such a sweet person who had a very warm and comforting smile all the time. A smile I would look for in times when I needed reassurance.

The furniture in the kindergarten classroom was very small; there were several light green long tables with their respective benches for chairs. I remember I was placed at the corner of one of them. The only recollections I have once we were inside of the classroom on my first day of school was of the bright sunrays that entered through the high-rise classroom window, and of the dust particles and **dragonflies** which were freely traveling under the sunrays. I do not recall any of the faces of the students in the classroom, in fact on that day I do not remember even having heard anyone talk. In my memory it was as if I was by myself in the classroom.

Just as the night before, there was too much excitement for me during my first day of school. My eyes before this day had never seen so much happening. At the end of the day I went to the area by the school entrance where the pupils would wait for their parents to pick them up. I looked and I looked to see if I would see my mother or father, and then I recognized the pale-rose outfit my mother was wearing that day—an outfit made of silk. She was raising her hand for me to recognize her. Good thing my mother was taller than the other parents for it was easy for me to spot her among so many people.

I was very happy to see my mother. In a way, I felt relieved after having lived what seemed a long time within a short school day. I never told my mother of this clear memory-impression I have of her. The memory of my mother on my first day of school remained with me as clear as if I had recorded it on a movie film. The camera back then were my eyes and the recording device my memory, for I, to this date can close my eyes and retrieve from memory this particular moment of my life and I can vividly see my mother.

The second day of school my father drove me to school and on the way back home I was to take the school bus. The bus chauffeur's name was Mr. Manuel, accompanied by Mrs. Raquel, a hazel colored eyed, mature woman who had a pear-shaped, white birthmark on her right arm. Don Manuel seemed to enjoy his job as a driver for he was always talking and laughing.

I started kindergarten with a group of students who would be my friends for many years. Although, I was very quiet when in kindergarten, I was able to make friends and for some reason I attracted Irene, a hyperactive girl, who every single day of school would not be apart from me. She in her entirety was as funny as her curly hair. Irene and I had some kind of special energy in common; a form of energy which was visible on her and kept hidden within myself.

My favorite game at school was when we used to sit and slide on the well shined, slippery stairs of the old school building. We would take our shoes off and with our socks made the stair steps more slippery. During the first part of the days, my uniform was impeccably white. My hair was well done. Right after the stairs play time, I was kind of a mess, then it was time to go back into the classroom when and where Irene and I would jiggle out of nothing, of course when Mother Clemencia was not watching us.

A Touch of My Eyebrows

The architecture design of the old school was Spanish. There was an inside terrace where we would line up each morning before the commencement of our classes to sing the national anthem followed by a prayer. I felt very much tiny when I would look up to the third floor's high-rise tile roof. Above the third floor, there was a wooden made annex where the dining rooms were. Our meal at school during lunchtime consisted of a delicious letter soup before the main entree. We used to spell our names and have a great deal of fun playing with the letters in the soup. When the main entree was served, we would eat very fast as to buy time, for right after lunch it was playtime. One of my favorite side dishes at school was fried yucca—the root of a plant which is eaten like potatoes. The first time I had this dish at school I happened to have touched my eyebrows as I was eating and placed my fingers inside my mouth. My fingers tasted salty same as the fried yucca. Ever since that moment and for many years to come, I complemented a fried yucca dish with a touch of my eyebrows, followed by the taste of my finger.

Extremely Quiet

As early as preparatory, the school year right after kindergarten, the nuns called my parents for a meeting. Their concern was that I was different. I guess the psychology of those days was not a careful one, for I heard when the nuns asked my mother if there was anything wrong with me, for as one of the sisters said it as she referred to me: "The little girl is strange" all that I did to be called "strange" was to be extremely quiet. In the classroom picture takings, all I did that year was to refuse to hold a doll when posing, when the rest of the girls did.

As the school years were passing by, my parents were called in for meeting with the nuns again and again for the same reason. What were the nuns trying to tell my parents? What did my parents want to listen or not to listen? I guess the nuns could not handle the fact that I continued to be extremely quiet and serious. What they did not know is that the serious expression in my face was a façade to hide a world of misunderstanding. My escape from those moments was for me to look away, and if near a window my escape was to look all the way through the window, with the hope of seeing the dust particles and the **dragonflies** as clear as I saw them on my first day of school when in kindergarten.

I was a good student but not one that would remain silent when it was that I was not satisfied with answers given to my questions. In religion classes, my mistake was when we were told that God was the first form of existence on earth and that God came from the nothing. To that I replied by asking what "the nothing" was and who had created "the nothing," and I was not satisfied with the nun's answer because in my young mind I would close my eyes and imagine "the nothing" as something dark and therefore as something that existed before God. Great shame I caused to my parents.

Greenery Yards of the Rich vs. Soiled Yards of the Poor

As the school days and years were passing each single day, I would go to bed wishing for the next morning to arrive fast so I could go back to school. Nothing could beat the feeling of waking up and getting ready just to go to school. My oldest brother Roger, my father and I would have breakfast and then rush to his Ford Falcon—a station wagon which he later replaced with a Land Rover jeep. The trip to school was very pleasant.

Secing Managua at that early part of the morning as it prepared for the start of each day was an event in itself. As we drove, I remember passing through affluent areas, smelling greenery on the recently watered front yards of the rich, and smelling soil on the recently watered front yards of the poor. The newspaper boys were shouting on the streets to sell 'La Prensa'—the daily newspaper, street vendors preparing their vintage-merchandise. School boys and girls wearing different uniforms were on their way to school.

My father paid attention to everything and would not excuse anyone we saw on our trip on the way to school, for my father would make a comment about each and every person or thing he saw. Laughter was part of our daily morning trip on the way to school, not to mention he would talk to me about the nuns in school assigning the nuns funny names, somehow naming them with a name close to their real names.

Soon enough we arrived at school to hear my father's last joke as he said good-bye, to continue his trip for a couple of blocks more to get to the Ministerio de Economia where he worked.

Alfredo

My family was growing bigger, my brother Alfredo was born in 1965. I have heard that in every family there is a clown. My parents brought home that day a large baby boy, who was smiling and who has never stopped smiling ever since. He was the cutest and funniest baby boy I had ever seen. Who do you think was back with us when Alfredo was born? Theo, the best thing about having Theo with us was that she was a person who could control Roger, my oldest brother who would the great majority of times misbehave and bother each member of our family. Unbelievably, Roger listened and obeyed Theo more than he obeyed my mother. This was a great relief for me and for those around me.

Piano Duet

In 1968, Tamara started school. By the end of that year, she and I performed a duet at a piano concert in school. We were dressed alike wearing a light blue dress. As quiet as we were during our performance and when saluting the public, I recalled we both jiggled after giving our backs to the audience right before we sat and started playing the piano. I recall having my eyes wide open and my attention on the music scripts as we played the music. Tamara played the melody and I played the accompaniment. In no way did I turn to see Tamara for I knew we would laugh and we could mess things up. The good thing was that the songs we played came out perfect. We were very happy, same as Mother Paul our piano and singing instructor. Our parents were very proud and happy. Right after our performance and before the piano concert was over, Tamara and I went to slide at the stair steps. It was so funny because the piano concert was on the first floor of the school and the piano was right under the stairs where we were sliding.

Ordered to Discipline Antoinette

I managed to get good grades in conduct during my first years of school. It happened that during the year I was in third grade I must have been sort of an example student.

For instance, I was ordered and given permission by the teacher to discipline my co-student, Antoinette. Antoinette was an American girl who was very insolent, we shared desks. Part of the authority given to me was to slap Antoinette in the face when she would not behave. As I was told this I recall having expressed a great deal of disconcert. Under no circumstances would I do something like that to a schoolmate I thought. I had lots of fun with Antoinette; in fact, she helped me to relax and to not be so serious.

Antoinette and I became very good friends. We used to make drawings of the instructors doing funny things. One day Antoinette showed up in class with a paper bag covering her head. Antoinette had gotten a very short haircut and she was embarrassed to enter the classroom. Antoinette's face was as red as the color of our uniform's skirt. I could not stop laughing, in fact that day I was the one, who according to the instructor, needed to be slapped on the face. We managed to make it through third grade with no problem and yet had a great deal of fun. My circle of friends was getting larger; imagine what it was like to have had Irene and Antoinette as my best friends. I later added Graciela and Celia as my friends during the years to come. Laughter, and more laughter was part of growing up. My group of friends at school was very popular and likeable at school by the nuns, teachers and by the students.

Child Abuse

My life so far was full of happiness everything around me was goodness until the year of 1968. I was eight years old. My mother's brother who was a teenager and who was visiting our house took me to my parents' bedroom. He told me that he wanted to learn how to dance with girls and told me that he wanted to practice dancing with me. We were standing up and he embraced me. Then he placed me in my mother's bed and told me to lie down on top of him. I was eight years old at that time, but it was the type of eight years old where malice was not present. I did not know what was taking place or what sex was. The good thing is that soon enough and right after my mother's brother had told me to lie down on top of him, my mother entered the room and saw what was happening, she screamed and hit her brother and she told me to go to my room.

Without me knowing why, at that time, my mother told me to bend on my knees next to my bed for hours that afternoon. I did not know what was taking place; I was not aware that I was doing something improper. I cried, I cried, and I cried. I even recalled the night got its way in and I continued to be on my knees without turning my bedroom lights on. Neither my mother nor I ever brought up the subject.

Of that same year, I have recollections of someone playing with my private parts, as I was half sleep. The lights were turned off and I could barely see that person's face, but I was more sleep than awake, it was as if I was drugged. A few times I have gone back to this moment in my life and I try to recognize who the person molesting me was. That person in my recollection had lots of hair. That person looked like one housemaid we had; this housemaid was very playful all the time. The house where we grew up was a two-story house. This housemaid used to jump the thirteen stairs from the second floor all the way down to the first floor in one jump. When I had tried to make recollection of this person at times I had panicked because the person molesting me could have been my uncle. Once again, psychology back then was not very open; parents did not talk to their kids openly as they do nowadays about child abuse.

The Child God

With the passing of the years, many Christmases went by. I remember going to school with large bags full of presents for my instructors even presents for Mr. Manuel—the bus driver and for Mrs. Raquel. My mother was very good at this, she never forgot anybody. Christmas Eve was always celebrated at our house where all of my relatives would come and get together. For some reason my family was one that attracted other relatives during the Holidays. On those nights before midnight, we would go outside of the house and for a tropical country, miraculously every Christmas Eve, a cloud would be passing by a bit before midnight.

We did not believe in Santa Claus, we believed in the Child God. Our father would tell us that the Child God was inside the cloud with lots of presents for the kids who were good during the year. In the meantime, my mother would place the presents inside our bedrooms. I believed in the Child God each Christmas until I was nine years of age. I was very sad for having had lost the belief in the Child God. The waiting of Christmas Eve was so special that I felt I lost a great deal by having learned, that my parents were the ones who placed the presents in our bedroom instead of the

Child God. I guess this was a part of me not wanting to grow up. I simply refused to do it.

I Heard a Commotion

I recall a day, having come down the stairs ready to go to school when I heard a commotion coming from my grandparent's bedroom—the couple who raised my mother. My grandmother was lying down in her bed and was having difficulties breathing. My mother was giving her CPR as my grandfather was standing by the door and watching. I was standing right behind him. My grandmother ceased breathing while I continued to watch without showing any emotions and without moving. My grandfather desperately left the bedroom and went to the living room where he cried as loud as a child would. I did the opposite, as my grandfather went to the living room, I entered the bedroom.

My mother held her tears at that moment for she was more concerned about my grandfather's wellbeing. My mother stepped out of the bedroom to be with my grandfather and when I was by myself with my dead grandmother, I took advantage to pull one of my grandmother's white hairs from her head. The next thing I did was to place that hair together with a piece of one of my grandmother's clothing inside of my dictionary of Castilian Spanish synonyms.

I carried that dictionary almost throughout all my school years and would at times just look at my grandmother's hair. I guess I kept my grandmother's hair for at least twenty-five years before I took it out of the dictionary and placed it in what I thought was a safer place; a place so safe that I forgot where I hid it. As I write I still carry the same dictionary with me. I do not recall telling anyone about my grandma's hair. I do not recall ever crying for my grandmother. The meaning of death was never explained to me. In fact, I assimilated everything I needed to learn about life outside of a classroom setting, through living and interpreting my own experiences.

Later that morning, Dona Esmeralda—our next-door neighbor took me to school to excuse my sister and I from attending school that day. Then next thing Dona Esmeralda did was to rush to a tailor's shop from where I walked out wearing a black and white polka dot dress. The burial of my grandmother was on the same day she died. There were no vigil services for her. Within a few hours, there were many relatives in our house. My grandmother was beautifully dressed in a beige dress; the dress she had once said she wanted to wear at her burial.

The next thing I recall was that I was standing by the main door of our home awaiting the exit of the coffin. My godfather was leading the way, stopped for a moment, and instructed the morgue people to turn the coffin around for under no circumstances would he allow for my grandmother be taken out of our home heads first. He said that if she did, we soon would have another death in the family. They turned the coffin around and my grandmother's feet were the first to come out of our home. There I was on one side of the coffin while my godfather was at the other side.

We drove from Managua to Diriamba in a caravan as we carried my dead grandmother to the cemetery. Diriamba, was the city where my grandmother was born and where she lived most of her life. Strangely enough the next person to die in our family was my godfather—the very same person with the superstition on the day my grandmother died. There were many men from the military the day at my godfather's funeral. He was a high member of the military of the then Somoza's regime in Nicaragua. For some reason I do not recall having felt any pain or mourned on any funeral I ever attended. I respected people's pain and would keep quiet but I would never shed a tear. I never really took the time to think about death, I was not afraid of it either.

Stopped the Clock on My Mother at Thirty-Six

The worst of my worries throughout my childhood was not about death. Strangely enough, my main worry was to think and to imagine that my mother could one day become obese. My mother has been and still is a slim woman. I worried and cried for nothing all of my growing years. I related obesity with aging. The fear behind was for my mother to never grow old. For years, when someone would ask me, how old my mother was, I answered thirty-six—I had stopped the clock on my mother at that age.

As Sweet as Her Smile

I was very lucky at school for I was one of the students selected to participate in almost every event. When in fourth grade I recall the day, I was among the small group of students who went to Regina's house to attend her funeral. Regina was one of my classmates. Regina had died in an automobile accident. She was the third and the youngest dead person I had seen. The impression I kept from Regina after having seen her dead lying in the coffin was as sweet as her smile.

Catechism Classes

During the year of 1969, I was taking catechism classes to prepare for my first communion. This year the Immaculate Conception School moved to a new building in the surrounding areas of Managua. Our new school site was the largest and most modern in the whole country. It was situated right in front of the UCA—University of Central America.

On this same year, the house we lived in was being renovated. One afternoon the engineer in charge of the construction informed my parents that the house would not be completely built on time for the day of my first communion. The catechism class I was taking in preparation to give my first communion was at the same school but with the students of the annex school, which were low-income students who attended this school sponsored by the nuns. I was upset when my mother came into one of my catechism classes and told the nun that I would not be giving my first communion that year.

My mother and father wanted to have a big party for my first communion at our newly renovated house. I had no say in this; I just looked at my classmates and accepted what I had just heard. I was sad and , I felt as if I was abandoning

my catechism classmates who although were very poor girls
had lots of friendship to offer.

Happiness in the Form of Energy or Vice Versa

In the mornings, right before school started, I would go with my two best friends, Graciela and Celia to play at what was still a construction site at our new school. The most fun was the competition when jumping on the piled construction dirt and across the irrigation channels.

Sometimes when we got a hold of the volleyball court we would play with my volleyball, which I would bring to school. Graciela, Celia and I would stay after class to take piano lessons with Mother Paul. The third floor at the school was designed for the music classrooms only. Mother Paul was very strict. She used a walking cane and when she was very upset, she would at times lift the cane to reach us as we were running away from her.

I used to get up to date in the practicing of the piano at home. That year my parents brought home a beautiful tall YAMAHA piano. Since there was no communication whatsoever between me and my parents, everything my parents did, or gave to me and my siblings came as a surprise, but to me it was a double surprise when I learned that the piano was for me. My parents expressed their love to me and my siblings by having always been there and by giving us the best of things.

I noticed a great deal of change in my behavior at the age of ten years old. It was as if I had lots of happiness in the form of energy or vice versa. I would come up with all sorts of ideas and would act on them inviting other students to misbehave. I became a leader with many followers. I could also not stand injustices, and without thinking or knowing, whenever there was something which was not fair, I would react and manifest my emotions in a way or two.

I really started having problems with conduct. No longer was I the quiet, little girl, which was the reason for which the nuns complained to my parents in the past. There was more complaining to do, but this time it was because I was misbehaving.

Refried Cockroach for Lunch

A moment of speaking up is very clear in my mind on a day we were having lunch at the school cafeteria. The food trays were being brought to our tables and a tray containing refried beans had a quite large cockroach sticking up right in the middle of it. That thing was as fried as the beans. I was upset and my appetite was just as dead as the cockroach. I recall standing and calling the cooks and the nun in charge to complain about the cockroach in the beans. I even demanded my lunch money returned to me, which was not possible for our parents paid for our lunch on a monthly basis. I had to be the one standing up instead of an older student. I mean things of this kind were gaining me popularity at school especially among the nuns and instructors.

Another day after a recess time and before it was time to go back into our classroom the oldest—secondary students wanted to join the UCA-university students on a walk out strike they were having against the rising cost of milk. I, being only a fifth grader, stood a step affront together with the secondary school students and refused to go back to the classroom when ordered to do so by mother

Superior—the director of the school. There I was at the age of ten with inquietude for fairness.

My First Communion

My first communion was here, it was the inauguration of the auditorium at the new school building, and the event was sensational, lots of people. We were dressed in a beautiful, impeccable, white outfit. We had assigned seats up on the stage. I do not know how Irene managed to accommodate herself next to me. It was funny that even at our first communion day Irene's curly hair was still rebellious. As we were entering the auditorium, a woman waived from a long distance calling on my attention. She came down to hug me. It was Aunt Marcia who had arrived on a surprise visit from the United States, to be at my first communion. After the ceremony, we went to my house.

As soon as we got home, I dressed into a soft lilac dress with pearls for buttons. The party was very special, my first communion and the showing of our newly renovated house. The givings were beautiful, I still have the small and fancy stuffed animals that were given. My grandmother Victoria, a woman who loved me a great deal, placed an ad in the social section of La Prensa, the newspaper of Nicaragua. Everything was great but deep inside, I was sad for I remembered my classmates from the annex school of the year before with whom I was supposed to have had my first communion. However, this was soon compensated for right after my communion my aunt Marcia convinced my mother to send me to the USA for vacation that same year, right after school was over. Said and done toward the end of the year, I was on a plane destined to Los Angeles, California.

Aunt Marcia and Uncle Lorenzo were very hospitable. They took me to all of the amusement parks in Southern California. At the age of ten I still saw Disneyland as a dream come true. Well, I guess Disneyland is still a dream come true for people of all ages.

My First Attraction to Another Girl

The year that followed I was in sixth grade—a big deal to me; this was the last year of elementary school. This year was also the year I felt attracted to one of my schoolmates, her name was Rocio. I never gave it a thought I only knew I thought this girl was pretty and that I liked her. I recalled having taken a picture of her when we were in line on our way to recess. I was not very lucky when the roll of film was developed for the picture of Rocio came out with no head. I do not recall being attracted to any other girl during the rest of my school years.

Swimming

Swimming classes were great at the new school; I mean Graciela, Celia and I already knew how to swim. The instructor did not have anything else to teach us. We got away with doing what we wanted during the swimming class. I will never forget the day that I went to the side of the swimming pool where the elementary school girls were and I brought Tamara to the deep side of the pool. We were very happy, and we both got on the jumping board and jumped into the swimming pool. This was a risky experience for we were both laughing so much that we could not get out of the water. Graciela came to the rescue and got Tamara out. Of course, this happened in a matter of seconds and nobody knew what was going on, and so we just went as if nothing had ever happened.

As the years were passing by, my childhood wanted to go away but at the same time I did not want to let go of it. It is true I had my struggles but I did not have any complaints. Why would I want to give up the many years of fun? Aside the happiness I had while attending school I was very happy in my 'own world' at home. I am thankful for having had my parents and their unconditional love they had for me and my siblings. If there was any failure from their part in the way I was brought up I only know that it was not intentional and they were the best parents they could be.

Lots of Happiness at the Beach

We used to go to the house at the beach every weekend if we could and for every vacation. On the way to the beach, we would stop at our 'finca' the farm where we would play with the children of Mr. Aniseto, the person in charge of taking care of the farm. The farm was a ten hectares piece of land with a river going through it in the form and shape of an L. Once at the farm we would go horseback riding, swim at the river, run and eat homemade food from scratch made by Mr. Aniseto's wife. This was very funny, for we had to hear Mr. Aniseto's stories about thieves that would enter the farm and would steal the hens, fruits, and vegetables from our part of the farm only, since my parents had assigned them a small piece of land for them to grow their own hens and produce. "You will not believe it, Don Roger," he would tell my father, "the thieves only took the hens from your side of the farm and not ours." I guess simplicity is a rare and treasured thing to have.

We would then continue our trip and stop at the town of San Rafael del Sur to buy 'jocotes'—a Nicaraguan fruit. I close my eyes and I can almost feel as being there back in those times. Once we were at the ocean, we would help unload the jeep and as soon as we were done, we would run to the beach. If the tide was in, we went to our favorite part of the beach where there were no rocks. We would then wait for the tide to be out, and we would go to a place where there was a huge natural made swimming pool. That is where my father taught me and my brothers and sisters how to swim.

At night, we would go seeking for crabs or just simply would sit in the sand in a group—a group that at times would have close to or more than fifty persons, mostly relatives. My father would always lead, he would play the guitar, sing or he would just improvise a game. He always told us stories he would invent. My mother was the quiet type. She expressed her love to us through her caring in the form of making sure we always got the best of things.

Landed on Quicksand

We used to go for a ride on the coast and my father would let Roger and me drive. One time I drove as far as I could from the house and I ended up on quicksand. The Land Rover got stuck in the sand and the strength of the 4x4 transmission feature in the Land Rover was not enough to get us out. We got out of the Land Rover and saw how little by little the Land Rover was sinking in the sand. The next thing we knew was that the tide was in and was making the Land Rover move back and forth. My father and Roger ran to the nearest town and came back with two local residents who brought with them a pair of oxen. They tied both oxen with a thick steel cord and tied the cord to the Land Rover.

We were able to see how the waves hit the Land Rover and how the waves moved it from one side to the other. The Land Rover seemed so lightweight when it was at the control of the ocean waters. The strength of the oxen though was able to save the Land Rover. We called our relatives in Managua and before evening we were on our way back to Managua. My father had to go back to the ocean the next day to bring the Land Rover back to the city. The Land Rover had to go through a very special cleaning in order for it to get started again. It did get started soon enough for our next trip to the ocean. An adventure like this one is one that happens to a few only—or so I believe.

A Key on the Ground

I recall one afternoon we were taken on a ride and were driving in Altamira D'Este—a newly built residential place in the surroundings of Managua. My father stopped the car and we walked. My father pretended to have found a key on the ground and picked it up. "This key must belong to one of these new houses," he said as he approached and asked us to follow him toward the house where he found the key. Before he opened the door, I told him, "Papa we are going to get into trouble." He proceeded to open the main door to the house.

"This is our new home."—he announced. We were all surprised and started jumping out of so much happiness. We moved into our new home on September 23, 1972. The reason we moved was that my parents wanted us to live and grow up in a more well to do place in Managua.

Managua Nicaragua Devastated by the 1972 Earthquake

Exactly three months later, on December 23, 1972, two days before Christmas Managua the capital of Nicaragua was devastated by an earthquake. On the night of December 22, 1972 at around 10:00 p.m., we experienced minor but continuous tremors. We were already living in our new home. Our parents had just come back home from playing poker at Uncle Juan Jose's house. They called it quits early on their weekly poker night when they were accustomed to play until midnight. We went to sleep early and were told by our parents to sleep with our clothes on. We went to bed as in alert. On December 23rd at exactly 12:29 am we were awoken by a strong earthquake, things were sliding sideways as we were getting out of our bedrooms, we encountered my mother who was coming to get us but who could not reach to our bedrooms for she was being thrown sideways at the hall. As we made it out of our bedrooms, we found my father holding the keys to the front door and followed him out. My father was shaking and could not get the door open. My mother had to open the door.

In Nicaragua, the houses are made of concrete, so in emergency cases for earthquakes the advice is to evacuate the houses/buildings. We made it out and saw our neighbors. The kids from the whole block were placed inside our Land Rover, which was a large jeep, which could accommodate up to twelve kids in it. We were placed in the jeep for safety, and our fathers would hang from the Land Rover for due to the tremors the heavy jeep would jump endlessly. That night was like the end of the world to us. People were running, one could hear sirens from ambulances, fire trucks, the screaming of people. One of our housemaids' poor being came out of her bedroom in her underwear; my mother caught this and was brave enough as to go back into the house to get this lady some clothing. Since Altamira D'Este was a residential community situated at a higher altitude than the center of Managua, we could see how the sky was red for the whole center of Managua was destroyed, followed by fires that broke after the earthquake. Some relatives drove desperately in the middle of the night and came to our house. This included my grandparents on the maternal side who managed to escape the debris of their collapsed house with the help of my oldest brother Roger, who was spending the night there. We survived that night. In the morning my father took us on a tour of what was left of Managua, the capitol of Nicaragua.

Managua Day of
the Earthquake

Our tour involved visiting relatives, seeing some of our relative's houses destroyed and finding out that one of our cousins who was only nine years old had died. The night before the earthquake my uncle and aunt for safety reasons decided to have the whole family sleep in the living room so that they could be together, and sadly the wall next to where my cousin was sleeping fell down, killing her. As we continued our tour of Managua, we saw a couple of half burned bodies on the streets. We also visited the house of our maternal grandparents. Their house was a beautiful, large, colonial style house made of asbestos, and the entire house collapsed. The 'Challet Morazan,' our grandparents' house did not exist anymore.

Our tour ended by visiting the previous house we lived in. The house my parents had renovated in 1970, which we vacated just ninety days before the earthquake. As we approached the proximities of the house, we saw that the wall on the second floor on the east side of the house was missing. My father stopped, closed his eyes and expressed the following, "Bless God," he paused and continued to say, "material things can always be replaced but not a life." The house, which was the best in that neighborhood, was down. We were very lucky to be alive. Our tour also included visiting The Immaculate Conception—our school, which was recently built as the largest and best school in Managua, and which had collapsed into pieces.

We soon learned that the only persons inside the previous house we lived in, on the night of the earthquake were a child and a live-in housekeeper. Although the second floor's platform had collapsed forming a less than a thirty five degree angle, the child and the live-in housekeeper were standing next to a wall which did not go down together with the collapsing floor. The neighbors rescued them both. The fact that we moved out of that house exactly three months before the earthquake remained a mystery considering that our house had recently been renovated. I mean we had only enjoyed our newly renovated house for two years. The house was beautiful. It does not make any sense as to why our parents would decide to, having had built a huge house for us to live in, shortly thereafter move into another house. We moved three months before the earthquake, if miracles exist this must be one of them. We were to survive the earthquake.

USA Year After Earthquake

After the earthquake everything came to a stop in Nicaragua. It was as if Managua was placed on hold. They closed all schools; there was no commerce, so on December 24,1972 that is the next day after the earthquake Roger, Tamara, my cousins and I flew to the USA, where we remained for the whole year of 1973. In total we were seven cousins. We all stayed with Aunt Marcia and Uncle Lorenzo with the exception of Roger who stayed with our uncle, the one my mother threw out of our house in Nicaragua back in 1968 for attempting to molest me as a child.

Child Molesters Never Rest

Child molesters never rest I guess, for in 1973 when I was thirteen years old, and still residing in the USA after the earthquake, that same uncle told me one night to walk with him to the store, and so I did. As we were on our way, he asked me if I remembered what had happened between him and I back in Nicaragua. I said, "No," and got away from him once inside the store. I got back to Aunt Marcia's house before he did. He never brought up that subject again. As I write this, I feel repugnance toward that uncle and to the thought that I could have become his victim once again. Did I say that child molesters never rest? Two years ago, this same uncle sent me a friend request on one of the social media websites. I do not understand why he would want to be a friend of mine. I only know that I had never felt a void when it comes to have feelings for a person, but that is what I felt, a void, an emptiness and nothing else. I could not even feel anger nor pity toward him.

My Sister Karina – a.k.a.Terremotito

In 1973 my parents, aunt and uncle came to the USA to spend Christmas with us. My parents brought Karina with them—our new baby sister. There was a baby boom in Nicaragua after the earthquake took place, I guess people got closer after the recent devastation and babies were born. These newborn kids were called "terremotitos" that is "little earthquakes," so that was one of Karina's first nicknames. After Christmas, Roger, Tamara, my cousins and I all went back to Nicaragua, each with their respective parents.

High School Years

When we were back in Managua, things were very calm; our only duty was to go to school. No more helping with the house chores as we did the previous year when we were in the USA. My sisters and I went to a Catholic Academy, a well-known school where the daughters of the highest politicians went. The Immaculate Conception, the school we attended before the earthquake did not exist in Managua anymore. If we wanted to attend that same school, we had to drive to Diriamba. I was very happy at the new school; my cousins who have spent the year of 1973 with me while in the USA were also sent to the same school. My first year at the Catholic Academy was my first year of High School. I was very good in the class subjects which had to do with numbers especially Algebra, of course with the help from the private instructor my mom paid to teach me at home. I did poorly in language/writing classes. Maybe this has to do with the fact that I am a very slow reader and also to the fact that I have great difficulty when concentrating.

Insolence

At the beginning of my last year in High School, I had inherited a key by the previous graduating class, which was the key to the room where the nuns kept the class exams. As if we really needed it, the keychain holding the key had a four-leaf clover inside of it. The four-leaf clover is a variation of the common three-leaf clover and it is considered to be a good luck amulet. So, one of the most exciting things we did at school, was to go with the aid of a flashlight to steal exams, on the nights when our parents would be entertained by some type of event taking place at school.

Once we were inside of the room where the exams were, we would light cigarettes and smoke to death. The things forbidden to us were the most exciting. What was more fun was when on the next day, I would stand on top of a desk and threat the good/do not break a dish type of students when I would announce that we had the quarter's exams, and that we would share these with a condition that no one would score a 100% so that we would not be caught. Of course, those good students would comply and so that is how we did it for the grades, especially I needed these grades for the non-number subjects. I could not help it but I continued to fail in conduct.

One of my favorites of misbehaving was to sit at the school corridors with a friend or two and to imagine things in-group. I was so creative that I would make them feel as if what we were imagining was real. We really got high without the need to use drugs. Soon after, we would just sit and laugh at our creativeness. We would go to the school's chapel and we would drink the wine and eat the hosts from the sacristy. Of course, we never ate the blessed ones.

Expelled from High School

Once I was expelled from High School. Our Spanish classes were taught on a bungalow section of the school. These bungalows were made of wood and it would get very hot inside of these classrooms. The Spanish instructor was not one that I liked much, perhaps it had to do with the subject I was never good in language/literature. Anne was a girl who had all of her life lived in the United States and had moved to Nicaragua recently. I guess her body was not used to the high temperature and humidity-typical of the weather in Managua.

As the Spanish class was being taught Anne expressed as if thinking out loud how hot the temperature was. Excuse me—but it was as if the instructor was offended or something. She turned her back from the blackboard, scolded, and ridiculed Anne. It was as if the instructor was reading a sermon or something. Anne started crying and out of nothing and without thinking I reacted telling Anne—in what I thought was a soft voice, "Do not cry for that son of a…" referring to the instructor. I grabbed my things and told Anne to do the same and to follow me. We both left the classroom. It happened that the instructor heard me and before we exited the classroom, the sermon was directed toward me. She then told Anne and me to wait for her at the director's office. I can understand me being expelled from school but I found it as nonsense the fact that Anne was also expelled. I stayed home for two weeks. I really missed school and my friends. It was very boring to spend the weekdays at home.

The day I came back to school after I was expelled, a group of nuns were right at the entrance of the school. As I entered the school the nuns showed happiness and expressed a great deal of affection toward me. I gave the same in return. I do not know if I should laugh now but guess who was watching from not too long of a distance— the same instructor who got me expelled from school. She was steaming from anger. I did not pay much attention to her. I was so happy that day for returning to school that nobody could do anything against my happiness.

Parents Called to a Meeting in High School

One afternoon, Sister Brenda told me she wanted to speak to me in private. We went to one of the empty classrooms. She was very kind in the way she spoke to me, though I really do not remember the details of the conversation. The only thing I remember is that it had to do with my behavior. I also remember that throughout the conversation she had my hand held in hers. She asked me many questions to which I answered with mostly questions of my own. I felt very good as she was talking to me. At the end of our conversation Sister Brenda told me to tell my parents that their presence was needed in school.

When I told my mother, she reacted by scolding me before she even knew what she would be told. I guess it was normal for her to think that something was not right at school one more time. I later found out that my parents were questioned if I had some type of a problem because they did not know what my behavior meant.

I only knew that I always did or tried to do what was expected of me. I knew my homework was to go to school and to do my best at it. I knew that whenever I did well my parents rewarded me. I knew I was smart for I did very well with numbers. I knew that I would go to the university right after High School. I knew all of these but I continued to fail in conduct. I could not help it that was the only way I behaved, badly.

The Sandinistas were Gaining Power

The Sandinistas were gaining more power in my last year of High School in 1977, and as soon as I graduated, I was shipped to the USA I say shipped for nobody asked me if I wanted to go. I came to the USA and I did not like it. I cried a great deal and I went back to Nicaragua. Two weeks later, I was shipped to Puebla, Mexico so that I could study Medicine. It was fun there for we would wait for our monthly checks from our parents and we would party hard, in a good way though. We would travel to nearby cities, eat, and get to know Mexico. Of course, because of the partying I did not pass the Prep school at the University. I communicated with my mother and told her that there was a way I could be accepted at the University in the form of negotiating, but she said she did not have the face for bribing.

One More Time I Was Shipped to the USA

Oh well, back to Nicaragua and in less than a month I was shipped back to the USA together with Roger for my mother did not want us to get involved in the revolutionary movement. This was a very dark side for me, I was here to stay. For the first time in my life, I felt very lonely, very sad. I missed my family a great deal. It was different to stay in the USA than to just visit. It was no more fun. I met all kinds of people, good and not so good. I would write to my parents and miss them.

Due to Major Depression and on top of that, since I had to deal with the fact that I was coming out of the closet as a homosexual, I sought the help of a psychologist. I know that I had to know what a homosexual was, but when it came to me being homosexual it was a different story. I thought I was the only homosexual in the world. I was able to deal with my issues at that time and remained in the USA.

During that time in 1979, they gave a special permit for Nicaraguans to work. I got a permit and I got a job at a fashion manufacturing plant.

Homeless People in the USA?

I recall that while I had my first job, I lived by the LAX (Los Angeles Airport) and I had to drive to a city which was about half an hour away by car. I in turn took three buses to get to work. In the mornings, when I left home to go to work it was still dark. When I returned home it was already dark. One morning, as I waited for the first bus at the bus stop, I was approached by a homeless person. He did not say anything to me, he just looked at me and then he spit in my head and continued walking. I do know that I was very sad, returned home to take another shower and took the day off from work. I recall sleeping all day long without telling anyone what had happened. I had never thought there were homeless people in the USA. In the next couple of days, soon after this incident I decided to buy myself a moped. I bought a light green PUCH moped. I had lots of fun while I had the moped. I remember I filled up the gas tank with seventy-five cents-I mean not even one dollar, and the gas would last me the whole week. Lots of savings and lots of fun as I drove it and the best part was I no longer had to stop at the bus stops.

1979 – The Sandinistas took Power in Nicaragua

Back in Nicaragua, the Sandinistas took over the presidency in Nicaragua in 1979.

1979 – Death of My Grandmother, Victoria

A few days right after, I was at work. One afternoon as I worked, I spoke with a woman from Nicaragua about my grandmother Victoria.

I went home right after work that day and I was by myself when I heard the phone ring. I picked it up and it happened to be Uncle Octavio from Nicaragua, he greeted me and without answering him, I went on to ask him what had happened to my grandmother. This was one of the strangest moments in my life. My grandmother was not sick that I knew of. Why would I relate the phone call with my grandmother? Uncle Octavio did not answer my question and told me he would communicate me with my mother. As soon as my mother was on the phone I asked her, "What has happened to my grandmother?" Her reply was that my grandmother had passed away that very same day.

I stayed in the room I was sleeping in for days. The good thing was that a holiday was coming up and therefore I had four days off from work. I gave myself permission to let myself go on crying during these days. My grandmother on the maternal side, the one that was my friend for life was gone.

After the four days of crying, I went back to work and placed my grandmother's death apart. From that moment on, I held on to my grandmother's memory as not letting go of her.

In a way, I felt as if my grandmother was with me and laughed with me. I did not let go of my grandmother for a long time. In fact, I, once out of curiosity went to a psychic—a palm reader from Cuba and she told me that I was alive because my grandmother, who was dead remained always beside me to protect me.

Family's Trip to
USA Delayed

My father had always worked at a government job and retained his job after the Sandinistas took power; however, he had many altercates with the Sandinistas at work which cost him his health. My father had a heart attack and my family's trip to relocate to the United States was delayed. To be hospitalized in Nicaragua right after the war was not the best of things to do. A relative of ours who is a doctor told my mother that there was not enough care for the elderly in the hospitals.

The medical attention was given to persons in the military. My mother sought the medical services of the best cardiologist in Managua. This doctor brought and installed all the medical equipment needed to treat my father in our home.

My Family Relocated to Miami Florida

In 1981 once my father was back on his feet, my family left Nicaragua to never return to live there. They relocated to Miami, Florida where they lived for exactly one year. My mother asked me to move to Florida to live with them. I told my mother I did not want to move to Florida.

Oh My God! Time for Me to Come out of the Closet

Oh my God; it was time for me to disclose to my mother that I did not like the opposite sex, a more than six-hour phone conversation. Where I recall the great majority of the time, it was silence from the other end of the line.

I told my mother I could not live in Miami. Right after the war there was a recently established Nicaraguan community in Miami, which for the most were people we knew and I told my mother that I did not want to be singled out by these people for being a homosexual. So instead, my family moved to California.

Disclosing My Sexual Preference to My Father and Siblings

The next day, my mother called my father, my brothers and sisters to the table for a meeting. My mother told them I was a homosexual. My mother told me there was a great deal of silence at the table. Their meeting ended when my brother Alfredo asked my mother if I had a penis. I mean, we must have known as we were growing what a homosexual was but I guess we did not have anyone in the family that we knew of to be homosexual. After that, my father, brother and sisters were all OK with my sexual orientation. My sister Tamara even helped me with certain things, in the form of giving me advice on what girls used to like and not like each time I would go out on a date. Tamara and I were always very close ever since.

My Little Sister Was Not My Little Sister Anymore

I took Tamara to work with me at the manufacturing plant where I worked. For good or bad she met her second husband. At first, she married Maurice with whom she had her first child Lorena. Her first marriage did not last long; they divorced.

Later she married her present husband. Oh well, my little sister was not my little sister anymore, she matured faster than I did.

Denise – My First Living Companion

While my sister Tamara was happy in her marriage so was I in my marriage I could say. I lived with Denise for ten years, lots of happiness during the first seven years of our relationship. We both loved and cared very much for each other. I remember I would be at work and I would call Denise to pack our things because we would go on short term trips very often to Baja California, and other places in California. We loved camping.

The last three years of our relationship was nothing but routine for both of us. The only thing left between us during the last three years of our relationship was loyalty. Out of respect for each other, even though we did not love each other anymore, neither Denise nor I spent a night outside of our home on our own.

My College Years

For a long time, I have been taking classes on a part time basis at the Long Beach City College. After a while I decided I wanted to attend school full time for otherwise it was taking me a lifetime to attain my college degree. I went to Rio Hondo College for two years. Rio Hondo College is in Whittier California. I loved that college. It is up in the hills and there are lots of trees. It was beautiful to see Rio Hondo College especially during the fall season. After two years I graduated from Rio Hondo College with an Associate in Science degree in Business Administration with concentration in accounting. My level of education at the time was perfect for an accounting position. I worked as an accounting clerk III for one of the local High School Districts. My coworkers were mostly elderly ladies. They were fun and good to me during the whole year I worked there.

California State University, Los Angeles

I decided I wanted to go back to school on a full-time basis to complete my Undergraduate studies. I attended the California State University, Los Angeles and completed a Bachelor of Science degree in business administration with concentration in accounting. I also obtained a minor degree in economics.

Denise Decided Not to Follow Me

Right after I finished my studies at the University, I got a job at one of the California State Agencies. I had placed a deposit on an apartment and when I thought we would be ready to move Denise said she would not follow me to my new place. The person I thought would be with me for life gave up on me. During the next three months, after the breakup of my relationship with Denise I ate saltine crackers and diet Pepsi only. Soon thereafter in a way, I felt relieved with the end of that relationship. I would no longer have by my side an unhappy person who would complain at each and everything.

I continued to live and do well in my job. Soon enough I was dating someone else. To my surprise my ex-partner Denise, came to knock at my apartment's door. I opened the door, did not let her in and told her I was already dating someone new.

Northridge California Shaken by the 1993 Earthquake

1993 was also the year of the Northridge earthquake, oh my God! As if, I had not been through the experience of the Managua earthquake. I was living in Sherman Oaks at the time, I had a studio apartment. Another night I was awoken by a devastating earthquake, things were not sliding this time around. This earthquake was all jumps, cracking of the walls. Furthermore, I had to put up with the alarming screams from the African American woman who lived upstairs who was screaming, "Oh my God, the kitchen floor is cracking…" Oh my God…Listening to her was worth than the earthquake itself.

The building where I lived was destroyed. I spent the next two days on the street right outside my apartment in the company of my neighbors. Since I thought that this earthquake was the "Big One" we expect to one day have in California, I did not bother to contact any member of my family, who were living in a city nearby. After a week or so my family informed me that they were worried about me for they could see and hear the television news of the surrounding areas of the earthquake's epicenter; therefore, they made me feel like trash for not having contacted them.

My Sexual Preference Disclosed by a Co-Worker

In 1994 I had problems at work with an African American co-worker who was not very decent with me to disclose my sexuality in front of other co-workers. I had decided that I would keep my sexual orientation private throughout my career. Right before I started this job as an accountant, I bought about five thousand dollars in suits and shoes appropriate for my career. I had told myself that since I sacrificed a great deal of things to obtain my career and since on top of this studying accounting was not the easiest thing I have ever done, I decided I wanted to look as a professional in order to gain more respect from clients.

The incident I had with this co-worker named Karl took away part of my dream, part of my profession, part of my appearance. I used to work in the old typical type of government agency building in Los Angeles. We worked in a large office where there were many tables. No one had an assigned seat.

Aurora, a co-worker of mine who had an earlier schedule than most of us would each morning sit on a desk by the window. I have always had a passion for windows. It was at work where I noticed that it was when seeing through a window and focusing on a particular object, that I would concentrate at my best. Though the opposite happens which I do not understand as I have also used windows all of my life to remove myself from difficult situations. Back to the bad incident in the office, Aurora before she would go to one of our clients would make a signal to me in order for me to sit on the table by the window she was occupying. One of those mornings the co-worker I just mentioned, was very upset because I got the table before he did. He stood in front of the table where I was and in a loud voice asked, "Are you a lesbian?"

I looked at him as if asking him to stop talking by just looking at him. He repeated, "Are you a lesbian?" this time in a louder voice. "I think you are" he said adding, "because you are always looking at the prostitutes out the window." I was stunned and shocked. He then blocked my way as I was trying to get out of the office by grabbing me by my wrist. He was very strong; I had to make force in order to pull myself away from him telling him, "Let me go!"

I went to the restroom and I only know that I will never forget that for the first time in my life I was crying out of fear and could not stop. The top Manager told me to take a couple of days off from work in order to rest and he also gave me a letter signed by him saying that harassment would not be tolerated at work while under his supervision.

Las Flores Mental Health Institution

One of the days which followed, as I was driving toward work without thinking I pull out of the freeway and changed my route and I did not report to work that day. I was embarrassed to go to work. I ended up at Daniela's house-a friend of mine. I was very depressed, my career which I was starting to build up seemed as if it did not mean anything. I was suicidal. I recall driving Eastbound on the freeway and as I took the off ramp toward the Southbound freeway one of the wheel covers came off my car. I stopped to pick it up and as I saw coming cars at such a great speed coming from the Eastbound freeway off ramp, I felt the air when these cars were passing by me, and I told myself "This is it." I was desperate and all I wanted was to end my life.

I proceeded to take care of what I was doing and by the end of the day and right at midnight I drove by myself and registered at Las Flores Mental Health Institution. As soon as I entered the hospital's lobby the old wall clock started counting midnight. This was frightening.

I had never been in a mental institution. All I know is that I was eager to end my life and felt that if I did not seek for help, I would kill myself. I recall having spent at least a week in that hospital where I slept profoundly most of the time with the help of medication. I was placed on disability. I was off from work for a couple of months for they gave me lots of medication and were regulating the effects of these on me. When I returned to work, I had to report to our new office building in a city near Long Beach. Karl was assigned to work in a different office.

Ricky

The day before I went back to work, I bought a Chihuahua dog for someone told me that pets were of great help in keeping company and in cheering one up. I got the most beautiful black and white Apple Headed Chihuahua. I named him Ricky and gave him my last name.

My experience of returning to work was one which to this date frightens me. I had forgotten what I did at work, I kept quiet about it and I remember reviewing every single note and every single literature I was given when I was hired. I also recall I had to review several audits in order to remember. Why was my job erased from my memory?

I recall one day as I was approached by Elena, a supervisor who asked me if I would like to work for her. I felt good and answered, "Yes." I guess the word was that I was doing a very good job. As soon as my former supervisor left work, I was transferred to this lady supervisor's crew. Having worked under the supervision of Elena was the best thing that had happened to me at work. Elena appreciated my work and was able to see that I had lots of potential for the job. I learned a great deal while in her crew and I performed my best. I worked intelligently and gave more than what was expected from me at my job as a way of compensating with what they had to tolerate in regard to my suffering on and off from Depression. At times I was on medical leave from work. I felt very safe working under her supervision. The issue of safety at work was a new issue to me. The key factor about this supervisor for whom I was able to give the best of me at my job was that not only did she see I had the potential for the job, most importantly she believed in me and in my work.

I was left on my own. I would do my work differently than that of the other auditors but the end results were good, and Elena never had any problem with that. In fact, the reviewer of our work at our office had said that I did things differently but that I was very good at what I did.

It was around this time that I took the accounting exam which is required in order to become a certified public accountant – CPA. I passed the analytical part of the test with the highest score which was 94. I remember we were given a real-life business case scenario where our job was to study the case; to find a way to solve the problem and to discuss and give recommendations to the businesses involved in order to avoid the problem in the future. The other three parts I did not pass for a few points difference on each part.

Daniela Loved Life More Than Anyone Else

During the year of 1995, my best acquaintance Daniela died from Cancer. This was very painful to me because I saw how she was being devoured by that malignant disease. The saddest part for me about Daniela dying was that she was the person who to this date I can say loved life more than anyone else on earth. Daniela was a person I met who helped me fight back against the deep depression I had fallen into right after the bad incident with Karl at work. After Daniela died, I no longer had a place to go where I could just sit or lie down in a sofa where I could talk, cry, to later laugh for she would make me laugh.

I remember on one occasion when I had no appetite at all Daniela called Martina, her next-door neighbor and asked her in front of me to convince me to eat. Her explanation for calling Martina was that since I loved femme women, she thought that Martina being a super femme woman, would convince me to eat. There was Martina holding a soup plate and a spoon looking at me and softly saying, "Eat, eat, and eat." Daniela's effort in calling Martina was not successful. By the way, Martina was a lesbian also.

Daniela told me she was worried about dying and leaving me to fight my depression by myself. She introduced me to a very femme woman Melissa; she said I would really like her because Melissa was the type of woman I was attracted to. Said and done, there was a match.

Melissa had a daughter. She was four years old. We loved each other very much.

My relationship with Melissa lasted two years. Melissa started distancing herself from me and I could not see it as it was happening. When I found out it was too late. Melissa called me after we broke up to tell me that her daughter would cry a great deal telling her that she could not live without me. I had to speak to Melissa's daughter over the phone. I told her that I had to leave because I got a job far away, and I told her that I would be coming back.

I spoke to Melissa many years after we broke up. She brought up things from the past and I did the same. We spoke about happy and not so happy times. On this conversation I asked Melissa if she loved me, and she said yes. I needed to hear this for when she did love me, I could not see it.

Please Take My Father in His Sleep

In September 1998, the sweetest person in this world died; a very painful loss, but I handled it okay. My father's health started to fail when he was sixty-seven years old. His kidneys were failing and we-that is my family and I decided to have him undergo dialysis treatment as opposed to submit him to a surgical procedure. This we did because we thought my father would not make it alive through surgery. Three years later as my mother was coming back with my father after one of his dialysis treatments, my father showed my mother the needle marks he had in his arms, and as he showed these, he expressed to her how tired and in how much pain he was for continuing to submit to that treatment. One morning during that same week I saw my father and stopped to think how much he had aged and how weak he had become physically. At that moment, I asked God to please take my father in his sleep so that he would not suffer any longer. Exactly two days later, I woke up to get ready to go to work and on my way to the bathroom I noticed my father was sitting with the lights off in the living room. I woke up my mother and told her that my father was sitting in the sofa and that it seemed he was not breathing. As we both approached the sofa, we confirmed that indeed he was not breathing and realized that my father had just passed away.

Tamara Attempted Suicide

My father's death had an unbearable impact on my sister Tamara. Two months later and on the day before Thanksgiving my sister Tamara attempted to commit suicide. We found Tamara in the bathroom. Her husband was at the house and said he heard a noise coming from the bathroom. Even though my sister did not succeed in her suicide attempt, life has not, is not and will never be the same at least not for me. After Tamara's suicide attempt came many years of a constant fight for Tamara's health. We were successful we had Tamara for many years after.

Diagnosed With ADHD

On February of the year 2000 I was diagnosed with ADHD and started a medical regime for this condition. The medical regime included medication, therapy sessions with a regular psychologist while at the same time I was also having therapy sessions with a psychologist specialized in treating people with ADHD. Lots of things were explained to me, I finally understood why until now I had lived a lifetime of asking questions, a lifetime of getting answers to my questions to soon again ask the same thing. I also learned the difficulty I constantly have with making mistakes and not learning from these, therefore repeating the same mistakes over, and over.

Salsa Dancing Classes
Oh Yes! Griselda Oh Yes

At about this time, I started going to Salsa dancing classes, oh yes Salsa! At the dancing class men learned the how to lead dancing steps and women learned the how to follow dancing steps. I was there to learn Salsa dancing as a lead person. On my first Salsa dancing class I asked the instructor if it was ok for me being a woman to learn the dancing steps which corresponded to men. The professor and the straight men and women in the class said they had no problem with this. If they would have had a problem I would not have stayed in the class. I was very courageous when young to take a class with straight people and to dance with the women in front of their husbands. Would I do this again at my present age? Not a chance. Later I learned that Salsa classes were being taught at the Gay and Lesbian Center in L.A. and I switched to the Center for my Salsa dancing classes.

Saturday nights I would go dancing to practice the dancing steps I had learned during the week. It was lots of fun for I would see the dancing professor and the other students at the same bar. What did my salsa dancing class bring me? I met Griselda a beautiful Puerto Rican woman who was a great dancer and to whom I dared asked to dance with me, with the few and only salsa dancing steps that I knew back then. She became an acquaintance of mine. She said I won her friendship by having had made her laugh so much when I imitated her feminine moves while we were dancing.

A Short Vacation Ruined by My Impulsivity

For some reason, each time I would see Griselda and when we got to go out on a short vacation trip to the local mountains, she and I behaved as if we had known each other for a long time. I treated her as I had never treated a woman before. I made her feel special; I invited her to have dinner while still on our trip. Once at the restaurant, I gave a diamond ring to the waiter for him to place it in her dessert. Everything went well we had a very romantic moment. The waiter brought chocolates in dried ice and hid the ring in one of her chocolates. Her reaction was a very happy one with tears in her eyes. She looked beautiful. Griselda inspired my poetry writing, I would out of nothing invent poems as I would just talk to her. Everything seemed right from the moment we left Los Angeles to go to the mountains. I think Griselda had never laughed as she did when on our trip to the mountains. On our way up the mountains as dark as the nighttime was, and without anyone or anything around I stopped my vehicle in the middle of the road, I raised the CD player's volume all the way up, played classical music, stood right in front of the car and pretended to be the director of an orchestra as I pretended to direct the music. That woman was laughing so hard that she was also crying as she laughed.

Everything was going well during our trip but the day after the very romantic night that we had, I acted and did something out of impulsivity. I opened the bathroom door when she was in the bathroom. I did this without any bad intentions. I did this without thinking. I just wanted to scare her. This was a childlike behavior of mine. She was not happy and asked me what was wrong, I told her that sometimes I act on impulse. My condition of ADHD came to the conversation and then she asked me if I was taking any medication for the condition. I replied that yes, I was taking Ritalin for this condition. Of course, there was a change in Griselda's behavior toward me, we still had lots of fun but I knew and felt the change in her and I knew at that time that I had ruined our trip.

A couple of months later, I saw Griselda at the same discotheque where I met her. She was very happy to see me, so was I happy to see her. It was a Thanksgiving weekend. The first thing she told me was that she had left me a message at work. Right away I asked her to excuse me and went to call my place of work to confirm that indeed she had left me a sweet message at work. After that she was embracing me, holding me and we headed to the dance floor. We danced to salsa music but in a very romantic way, that is in a very close way. At times we laughed and jumped as we danced out of happiness for seeing each other again. She also showed me the ring which she said she would never stop wearing until the day she dies.

I saw Griselda for a second time at the mall and when she asked me how life was treating me, I answered that life was treating me alright with only one exception, she was not in it.; meaning that she was the only part missing in my life. She then reminded me that I knew her number and that I knew where she lived. Griselda was still wearing the ring I gave her. After I met this Puerto Rican woman I, once again, promised myself that I would remain single for the rest of my life. I have heard that when we get to be old, we live from our memories. I am only forty-three years old and I feel that I could continue to live from just the memories I have from Griselda.

My Jeep Wrangler

During the month of December of the year 1999 and before Christmas I loaned my second vehicle—a jeep to my supervisor for his car broke down. One morning this supervisor got involved in an accident and almost totaled my jeep. Accidents do happen but he behaved very irresponsibly after the accident, including a sexual harassment pass he made at me. The sexual harassment was by this supervisor asking me to show him my hands, he then placed my hand in his hand and rubbed my hand front and back, as he was telling that he had watched a documentary on TV the previous night. He told me that according to the documentary the index finger in lesbians was larger than the second to the index finger and he told me, "Which is the case in you?" he released my hand and immediately said, "Come to my office." Dale wanted to determine if my fingers corresponded to what he had seen in the documentary. I felt disturbed and embarrassed by this experience.

The sexual harassment pass was making more sense to me each day. See, hands and intimacy pretty much go together among us lesbians.

On My Way to Self-destruction

I became very anxious and started acting on impulsivity big time. Once again, I ended up being hospitalized in the psyche unit again and again and again. Throughout my adult life up to now, at times I was hospitalized for private reasons and at times I was hospitalized due to problems at work. Yes, the place in which I saw my dream come true (my job), took away a great deal from me, little by little it consumed me.

I started going to Las Vegas. On my way to Las Vegas I would play music and cry all the way there. Once in Las Vegas, I would play the slot machines and my thinking did really go away. It was as if I was in a type of Disneyland for adults. I was on my way to self-destruction and the ending I had planned was to commit suicide.

Las Flores Mental Health Institution Again

I recall one night after a long weekend, returning home from Las Vegas where I spent all my check from work which was quiet a lump size of money. As soon as I came home, I got a few things ready and checked in as a patient at Las Flores Hospital, the psyche hospital I had been before. I was psychiatrically hospitalized for extreme depression and suicidal ideation. The next day while still in bed I called my supervisor Elena. I told her that I did not know what was going on and told her that I had awaken at the hospital. I was hospitalized for about three weeks.

I was suffering from a great deal of depression accompanied with anxiety. I had known what depression meant but when coupled it up with a great level of anxiety was different. The way it was for me was that I had reached a deep level of depression with a great deal of uncertainty and of acting on impulsivity. I did not know what I would come up with and act on it. This experience is what made me work just for a while with Elena once again. My psychiatrist at the time and my psychologist wrote to my place of work and asked them to remove me from the stressful environment I was in.

I recall being still in the psyche hospital when I received a phone call from Elena telling me that my place of work wanted to interview me for a promotion. It was kind of funny for I had to tell the patient I shared rooms with at the psyche hospital to allow me to be alone in our bedroom for a matter of at least one hour. I waited for the phone interview. As ridiculous as it sounds, I was being interviewed over the phone for a job promotion, by members of one of the State agencies in California while I was on my hospital stay at the Las Flores Mental Health Institution.

I was promoted as an associate/senior position at work. I want to think of this promotion as a gain, but in fact it was not a promotion it was that they removed me from the stressful situation at work.

The New Office

I felt very lonely at the new office and I missed the people from my previous office a great deal. The new supervisor at the new office shared with me his discontent for I was promoted from outside of their office. He told me that other people in his office could have gotten the job instead of me. After other incidents, I asked the highest person in our office to please change me from crews. He answered that it was the policy of their office, for employees to work under the supervision of a supervisor for at least one year before they would consider a transfer between supervisors.

Teresa Is a Girl
Oh Yeah Teresa Is a Girl

An older supervisor would tell me all the time as I passed by him that he liked the perfume I was wearing. One time he asked me the name of the perfume, I told him the name of the perfume and he said he would ask his wife to buy that perfume for her. On one occasion he came to my cubicle and in front of my co-worker he said, "Ah! It smells good oh yeah it smells so good. It smells like a girl," then turning to my other co-worker who were standing in the hall and saying, "It smells like a girl. Oh yeah, it smells like a girl because Teresa is a girl."

"Did you guys know that Teresa is a girl? Oh yeah Teresa is a girl." I felt humiliated once again.

As If There Was a Tomorrow for Tamara

During the year of 2000, two years after the exact anniversary date my sister attempted suicide I had to be with her. That night we almost rushed to the hospital as it seemed Tamara would be leaving us -I mean she would die. I could feel her bones as I caressed her to make her feel at peace and I for the first time-expressed love to her through physical contact. Surgery for the after math of her suicide attempt was here.

My sister Tamara asked me to go with her to the appointment she had with the surgeon at USC. Despite all of my ups and down, what I like about me having ADHD is that when I am able to concentrate, I guess I over concentrate. My responsibility with my sister, when with the doctors was to make questions, understand, gather and retain as much information as I could before, during and after the surgery. At the same time and in the best way I knew I gave Tamara the emotional support needed, no matter if I felt like dying inside. I hid it above all costs for she needed me. I always talked to Tamara as if there was a tomorrow for her.

I Continued on My Way to Self-Destruction

One day, out of nothing, I told Elena that if I was ever to die it would be of a natural cause. This I said to her because I was not feeling well at all. The situation at work did not get any better.

I continued to place myself in a self-destruction situation by going gambling again and by thinking that the solution to my problems would be dying, meaning contemplating the idea of suicide. I went to the psyche hospital for anxiety related problems for at least two times while still at work in the last office I worked at.

On one occasion, I called my place of work to report to work after three consecutive days of gambling. I was surprised for at that same phone conversation it was announced to me, that I was removed from my supervisor's crew and that I would be working for a new supervisor.

Soon enough, there were problems with the new supervisor. She was determined to fire me from work; she was the supervisor who was in charge of firing employees. Before any employee in our department would be fired they would be transferred to this supervisor's crew. However, things did not go her way with me for without her knowledge I contacted and asked help from higher up personnel. I was advised to document everything.

How Did You Make It Through High School and the University?

After a month of working for Brenda, I gave up and asked for sick leave. I was placed on disability by my psychiatrist during August of 2001. She was not happy about this and before I left, she showed her discontent by entering into an argument with me and asked me "How did you make it through High School?"

"How did you make it through the University?"

I told her that it took me a longer time to make it through school. Actually, until that moment when asked by her I realized that indeed it took me longer than others to complete my university studies. I recall that while I was attending the University, I did not even had time to go to a family BBQ. The excuse I used to give myself was that the career of accounting was very difficult and very time consuming.

The conversation with this supervisor ended by her making inquiries to me about my medical condition, and at the end she told me "Why don't you have your doctors tell us what is it that you have so that we can make the necessary accommodations?"

An Epic Poem

One night on October of 2001 while I was still on medical leave, I started writing a book. I wrote non-stop for two consecutive days and then put the book aside. I returned to work from medical leave in November of 2001. I continued writing my book on my first day back at work. My therapist explained to me that I worked during the day and at night I would release the tension from work through writing. She must be right for I remember that there were days when I had an urge to write. I was once told by a named person in the movie industry that "A Visitor Awaits You"-my book is an Epic Poem. This gentleman was moved to tears after reading my book. He wanted to help me with the publication of the book, he wanted me to meet a playwright he knew, but when this person wanted to help me, I was not ready for it. As it was explained to me, my book is probably the result of needing to find a relief from all I was going through. The book clearly reveals the state of mind I was in when I wrote it. The important thing about my book is that when I sent it to different literary agents, I got a response from two different agents. It is my understanding that literary agents receive thousands of daily correspondences and that the majority go unanswered by the agents. Although my book was not published, to me the fact that I was contacted by two literary agents was in itself a trophy. *A Visitor Awaits You* will be my next project to work on.

The Dragonflies in My Mind

My last return to work after being on disability was on November of 2001. I have been permanently disabled since April 2002 until the present time. I never returned to work, the doctors in charge of my mental health did not allow me to. I have received a great deal of medical treatment by different psychiatrists and psychologists.

I do not wish to elaborate any further with how my work situation evolved because it is very sad for me. It brings me lots of pain. This was the very crucial time in my life when something which was once real and later a hope, became a need. The first time I removed myself from a difficult situation when in kindergarten, the **dragonflies** I saw were real. Later when removing myself from a difficult situation I did not see the **dragonflies** anymore. I only hoped to see them. And the day came when I needed to remove myself from the worst situation in my life, and on this day, I felt a great need to see the **dragonflies,** leaving me with no choice but to close my eyes. And finally for the first time I was able to see **The Dragonflies in my Mind.**

Isolation

Living during the last four years has been very difficult for me. I have lived through all of the symptoms of Depression. The most prevailing symptom for me all of these years was crying at first until the symptom was replaced with 'isolation.' I isolated myself in my bedroom at my mother's house with Ricky-my Chihuahua dog by my side. Isolation, in my experience, is the worst of the symptoms of depression. To me it was debilitating and it still is. Part of my isolation started with the shame of not working anymore. Isolation for me was the point where I feel I lost my mind. I lived in isolation so intensely that I forgot about everyone and everything. Reason for my being alive and still thinking (in the way I do), is Ricky, the love of my life and my life-time companion. What I never stopped doing was to take Ricky for his daily walk at the park. He would get his way and in a language of his own, would remind me of his daily walk. On the days I felt the most depressed, Ricky would with more emphasis do all kind of moves and noises. He would walk on top of me, even on top of my head and got me awake. During the nights it was hard for me to fall asleep Ricky would look at me as if demanding that we went to bed.

What Happened? I Asked

In 2004, I reached for help. I went to a clinic, told my story and that day, I ended up at Grace Hospital at the psyche unit and I was kept there for about one month.

At my first psychotherapy session I told the therapist that I communicated better through writing for I did not want to talk. I noticed myself as I had noticed before that I used body gestures a great deal on that first appointment. It is as if by lack of words I made a language of my own or perhaps I was not used to hearing myself talk. I raised my arms and with my eyes wide open at the same time, I asked the therapist "What happened?" There are days when I still ask my therapist that same question. Her answer has been "Too much trauma."

It is very difficult for me to understand "What happened?" I was able to accomplish the most important dream I had which was to attend the University to become an Accountant.

I worked as an accountant and even sat for the CPA exam.

My memory has deteriorated a great deal. I have never told anyone that when in isolation I used to stand in front of the bathroom mirror and I would repeat the following information about myself starting with my name "Maria-Teresa del Carmen, Managua, Nicaragua, Catholic Academy..." I did this as to not forget who I was.

In regard to my memory, I noticed that it is through re-living experiences that my memory comes back. For example, my brother Alfredo and his wife invited me to go on a trip with them to Guadalajara, Mexico. It is very frightening to me because almost everything that I did in Mexico brought memories in me of: what I used to do, what I used to like to do, memories of having gone on vacation, in other words I for the first time thought and remembered that I was happy once and that I did have a life. We went to many different States in Mexico, and in more than one place I remember telling my brother...Alfredo, I have been here before. There must be a term for what I am trying to say, I remember by doing.

Living in My Car with Ricky My Chihuahua

I was very lucky all of these years after I stopped working because my mother allowed me to live in her house for free. Ricky and I had a room to ourselves all these years. My idea was that I would live at my mother's house temporarily, and once I could go back to work, I would get my own place. Well, it happened that I stood at my mother's house for many years contrary to what I had planned.

It was around October of 2004, one morning I woke up and got desperate to see my situation, no job, no place of my own, etc. I believe it is an indication that there is trouble when someone in their 40s is still living at their parent's house. I got all of my things and placed them in my car and took Ricky with me. I did not leave any note at my mother's house, I just disappeared.

A couple of days later, I called my psychotherapist and informed her that I was living in my car on the streets. She did not see this decision of mine reasonable. She instructed me to talk to my psychiatrist who in turn told me to check in at the mental facility.

Grace Hospital Psyche Followed by Board and Care Living

The first few days of my hospital stay I did what I usually do during my first three days and sometimes during my first week in the hospital. I slept all day for when I would be awake, I would not stop crying. As puzzled as I was, the next week I noticed a beautiful woman in about her fifties at the dining area. When it was time for us to eat, I would make sure I sat down next to her, until I finally asked her what her name was. "Marie."—she said with a big smile on her face. I presented myself as Teresa and smiled as well. Each time I found her I would follow her with my sight and never lost any detail about her doings. This I did in the most discrete ways or so I thought.

It happened that Marie and I became friends while on our stay at the hospital. She was what we call 'bi-curios' that is she liked the opposite sex, but she wanted an intimate experience with another woman.

After having had spent the day with Marie during the evening, I went back into my bedroom and a bit later Marie showed up by herself at my bedroom. I was sitting in my bed and she lay down in front of me in a fetus like position.

I embraced her with strength and tenderness at the same time, she thanked me and what I did was to continue holding her and caressing her head and played with her hair. This moment ended when one of the staff nurses came into the room as she was doing her supervising rounds. She told us that that type of behavior was not admissible for we were at a hospital. Once she left Marie made a comment telling me that we were not doing anything bad. Of course not, we were just being two human beings, yes two confused human beings. Whenever we had a chance that same evening, and during the days to come we would embrace each other.

One advice they give at the Mental Hospitals where I have been is to not make friends on the outside with people you meet at your hospital stay. Imagine that would be as two large issues or problems getting together. It is extremely difficult and so uncertain for me to live my life, so imagine if I bring to my life someone with problems like mine.

The next day, Monday I had to take care of business in relation to my living situation, which was not having a place to live in. My medical doctors had told me that I would not be released from the hospital until I found a place to live in. The recommendation of Dr. Alexis, Dr. Lee and Carol-my psychotherapy was for me to go from the hospital directly to a Board and Care place. A social worker called 'The Board and Care' and she made all of the arrangements for me to go there. Until now I had never known what a Board and Care place was, I did not even know these places existed. The way I understand a Board and Care place is that it is an assisted living facility for the ill. You are not hospitalized but you are really not living on your own because they provide you with meals, housecleaning, and they also administer your medications; though I have permission from my psychiatrist to handle my own medication.

Finally, the moment for me to depart from the hospital was here, Marie and I embraced each other with so much tenderness for we each knew that we would not see each other again. Also, Marie was to stay at the hospital for an indefinite amount of time.

My first impression of the Board and Care was that of a little community within a community with little houses all over the place. Each little house was a bedroom to be shared by two people. The owner of the Board and Care showed me the whole place and lastly the bedroom I would be sleeping in. I was introduced to Betsie my roommate to be. I said "hi" and shook hands with her. I looked at the bedroom and almost said, "No, thank you," but I remembered if I said no I would have to go back to the hospital. The doctors did not want me living on the streets. The room at the Lodge was very plain; a fluorescent light in the ceiling, two beds, a piece of furniture between the beds and a bathroom with a shower. The beds in the reclining part have wood nailed to the wall with two poles in each side also nailed to the wall. The bases of the beds are bunk beds. A means for the beds not to be removed, I guess.

On October 14, I wanted to relate a message to Marie but not over the phone so what I did was to send her flowers. It was a special order I had to make at the flower shop because the flower arrangement could not contain any thorns, wires, glass, or any material that could be used for patients to harm themselves. Marie called me on the phone and thanked me for the flowers and said that what I wrote on the card which was delivered with the flowers was beautiful. I told her that I did not know if what I had written was a poem or if it was just the writing of a crazy person. I lost the poem and I do not recall it either.

Unbelievably, for the first time I do believe in coincidence. On the day I started a daytime program at the psyche hospital, as I walked, I picked to take a look through the double door windows, which led to the area of the hospital where Marie was still hospitalized. I could not believe my eyes, for I saw Marie saying Good-Bye to the hospital staff, I could see her profile and as I was looking at her, she turned in my direction and saw me. I moved away as to give her privacy, but I stayed right by the door. Her sister came out first and seconds later Marie came out of the double doors, she was crying. I tried to approach her but withheld. The gift she left me with was that she stared right at my eyes as she walked; the only sadness was the fact that she was crying. I felt as a child in front of a cotton candy just looking at it without been able to have it.

Living at the Board and Care Facility

Living at the Board and Care is something else. It is as if you are in the desert in a very small community. We, the people at the Board and Care are mentally ill, some are very functional still and some are not each and every one with their own story. One thing I noticed is that people at the Board and Care are good hearted people. You do not see any bad intentioned people, you see simplicity. What we all have in common is that we are all living in poverty. The money for the people that receive assistance from the Government goes directly to the owner of the Board and Care to pay for the living expenses. I have been paying my living expenses from the money I receive from the Social Security Disability.

One day while at the Board and Care, I really had nothing to do and nowhere to go because I only had $1.46 in my pocket. It was really something to spend the rest of the month with that amount of money. The good thing was that at the Board and Care I for sure had food three times a day. Although I have never eaten food worse than the food they give us at the Board and Care. For lack of money thereby no place to go, one thing I did for sure was to listen to the stories of my roommate, a bald-headed woman in her 40s I had back then. I forgot to mention that I went to the supermarket and bought a banana and a plum. It cost me 0.37 cents. And on this same day I ended up listening to classical music and writing most of what you have been reading so far.

I have had different roommates at the Board and Care. At first it was Betsie, an African American lady in her fifties. She became mentally ill after her daughter was killed in the Los Angeles area. The second roommate I had was Channel, another African American lady who had come from New York running away from her three past husbands/lovers who according to her, used to beat her up all the time. Channel claimed to have had seven heart attacks. The third roommate I had was Jenny (the bald-headed woman) a married woman, who one day out of the blue and without telling her husband got on a Greyhound bus destined to Los Angeles, and left her husband in New York. She was bipolar, she talked all the time, I mean nonstop. It was funny for each morning she would awake and the first thing she would say is "The Lord told me...." And she would look at me waiting for me to laugh and she would also laugh. I mean every single morning. I did not have a fourth roommate because I am now living in a room by myself. The room is like a single apartment on the second floor on the West side of the building which faces a street with private homes in it. I also have a partial view of the mountains.

A Kiss on the Cheek

My first Birthday at the Lodge came, and I went to my mother's house because she said that if I did not show up at her house, she would not give me a Birthday present.

We went to a Buffet. I got my presents. My mother took advantage and finally had the excuse to hug me for a long time when she said Happy Birthday to me. I was stiff but padded her back a couple of times. After I saw the Birthday present, I got up from the sofa, approached her and gave her a kiss on the cheek. I guess Birthdays and Holidays are good days for physical contact with my mother.

An Assessment

Today, Saturday November 6th, I spoke with Daniel, a nurse from the long-term care insurance that I have. He came to make an assessment about me to see if I qualify for long term care paid by the Insurance. I was asked the usual questions regarding my mental state, which by the way seems to have deteriorated a big deal by now. I could not help it but as always, I cried during the assessment. I cried out of frustration when he asked me to tell him the highest level of education I had completed. I mean I did not go to the University all those years to become an accountant and end up disabled and living at a Board and Care place.

I started paying this long-term care insurance through my place of work since 1996. Back then I did not have the slightest idea that I would need this type of insurance especially at such an early age. I mean I am only forty-five years old!

My first Holidays at the Board and Care just passed by, Thanksgiving was good. I had a very good Christmas and so did everyone else in my family. The environment at the house where we met (that is my mother's house), was very peaceful. The food was great and the gifts much better yet. Everyone from my family was enjoying Christmas. The day before Christmas I went and took a box of cookies for each of the residents at the Board and Care.

Something As Simple As "You Don't Have to Talk"

As far as having a life as I did once, I have done lots of work with the help of my psychiatrist and psychotherapist.

At first, I was obliged to go to a once-a-week meeting at a center for Gays and Lesbians. I remember the first day I went to that meeting I was very nervous; my head and my neck were stiff. I was afraid to talk and one thing that helped me to be able to attend those meetings was that my psychotherapist told me something as simple as "You don't have to talk," so when I am not in the best of situations, I think to myself, *I don't have to talk*, and it relaxes me a great deal. When I started attending these meetings, I recall making lots of gestures with my eyes. There have been times at those meetings where I have been very quiet and times when I feel restless and I have behaved silly. The women in the group have many times said to me that I am very funny, hilarious, etc. What they do not know is that while I am behaving as if I was a clown or something I am on the lookout and watch myself for not getting too silly or out of control, because when I am being funny is when I am nervous, and these are the times when the psychiatrist adjusts my medications as needed.

Ricky Going from House to House

The Long-term care insurance approved my claim and started paying for my living expenses at the Board and Care in the year of 2005. They pay the living expenses equivalent to the expenses for two persons so that I can have a room of my own. It is true, I was relieved for my financial situation would improve a great deal; however, this in itself got things more complicated in regards to my Ricky. It was convenient for me to stay at the Board and Care after having been broke for a couple of years, but it meant that it was not in the near future that I could start looking for a place to live where I could have Ricky with me. I tried very hard to find a place where Ricky and I could live before my hospital stay before coming to the Board and Care. In the meantime, I had a lady who took care of Ricky during the weekdays. Another challenge for me right at this time was that the dog sitter (Ricky's babysitter or so) was going back to her country of origin, so meaning where would my Ricky go? I have placed the love of my life, my Chihuahua in a situation which he does not deserve, going from house to house before I met the dog sitter. I could see happiness in Ricky when I would pick him up from the dog sitter on Fridays and I could see sadness when dropping him off at the dog's sitter Monday mornings. Sometimes after I picked him up, once in the car I could see tears in Ricky's eyes. I decided that the best thing for Ricky was to put him to rest. That is to put him to sleep. On Friday the 21st of January 2005 Ricky ceased existing. He would have been exactly ten years old in just four days. Ricky was born on January 25th of 1995. He was pure bred. Ricky's father's name was Chirino Sanchez as written on Ricky's birth certificate.

The Saddest Day in My Life

I thought and I think I had referred to the saddest day in my life before but let me tell you that no day has ever been as painful as January 21st 2005 at exactly 3:15 pm when they took Ricky from my hands at the pound. I had Ricky in my left shoulder, I was hugging him and when the girl that worked at the pound came to take Ricky away, I grabbed Ricky at that moment and put him face to face with me and kissed him as I have never kissed him before. I kissed him with so much love all over his face and held him up and looked into his little eyes. The lady at the pound there made a gesture to grab Ricky and when that happened Ricky cried with lots of anger and moved and twisted his body. The girl said she would bring a leash and so she placed the leash on Ricky's neck, well Ricky did not move at all when she tried to pull him. The girl then said she would bring a kennel. It was very hard when all of this was happening, I mean Ricky was prolonging his life with his behavior, to me every second that passed by at that moment felt as if years were passing by. I was in so much agony same as Ricky. Before putting Ricky inside the kennel, I asked the girl if I could remove the leash she had placed on Ricky and she said yes. Once Ricky was inside the kennel and as the girl took him,

I did not lose sight of him for a while and told him, "It is OK, Ricky." These were the words I would say whenever it was that I needed Ricky to be confident and not afraid. I continued to say, "It is OK Ricky," until I lost sight of him.

I cried the rest of the day and I continued to cry for many days thereafter. The tears still come to my eyes when I recall Ricky, but I replace these with good memories of Ricky. I remember that Ricky used to get very sad whenever I was sad.

I called Carol, my psychotherapist, and I left her two messages in her voice mail telling her what I had just done with Ricky. I also told her that "I was going to be OK." Leaving this message meant to me that "I was going to be OK" meaning I was reassuring my wellbeing and this reassurance would stop me from going insane or from having suicidal ideations.

The following weekend it was Alfredo's Birthday. He had a party. I attended the party and kept quiet about the news that I had put Ricky to sleep. I did not want to change the happy mood of my relatives into a sad one. For I know they liked Ricky a great deal. But my question now, where was my family and why did they not help me with Ricky when I asked for the help so that I would not give him away or not put him to sleep? Who knows! I do not know.

Improving My Social Skills

I have been attending the group at the center for Gays and Lesbians on a regular basis now. I have noticed improvement in my socializing skills, but it has been very hard to get where I am and as I have said before I have done lots of work on the therapy sessions and on following my medical regime. I am very compliant when taking the medications that I need. I also communicate to the psychiatrist and psychotherapist everything that is happening with and around me. I am very honest with them and this I think helps for me to remain emotionally stable.

Recently I noticed that my interest in meeting other women that is my interest in dating is back. Fear is what had made me stop asking people to go on a date. My fear was that I used to think and ask myself who would want to date someone: without a job, disabled, living in a Board and Care place, living with ADHD and Major Depression and on top of that someone having a Mild Cognitive Impairment (MCI) which is the last diagnosis given to me within the last two years.

Beyond Her Understanding

Well, I still have the fears I just mentioned and yet I have asked two women out on a date within the last two months. LOL which means Laugh Out Loud in cybernetic language, none of these women said yes to my invitation, I mean they did not give me a chance to at least go on a first date out! In a way I am confirming that I was right in having all those fears preventing me from asking women on dates. The difference is that I have gained back the courage and confidence in myself which allows me to ask women on dates. I know I have quite a large list of red flags that alert people to say no to an invitation, but you know what? I do not care. I will continue to ask women to go on dates. I feel I have goodness and lots of love to give to the woman that would want to see beyond her understanding and be okay with this.

I have noticed that people are afraid of 'transparency' in a person. I know I am a transparent-crystal clear person; there is not much that a person has to wonder to get to know me. As from my experience, most of the people with mental conditions that I have met are transparent and keep their guards down. I just think that people in general are not at ease with people who have their guards down, because they do not know what it is like to live with their own guards down. I better change the subject because the more I write and think about what I am trying to say the more I will get into a labyrinth of words.

Anna

I have a love interest in Anna. Anna is the facilitator at the weekly meetings I attend at The Gay and Lesbian Center. She is a beautiful and a very sensual woman, and she knows this very well for it shows in the way she carries herself. I felt as if I was going to faint the night she came with a mini skirt and high heel shoes. I could not help it but that night I followed each and every move she made, and everything around her spelled sensuality on it, even when she turned her head and her hair followed. The last time I saw her I was able to see deeply into the beauty of her eyes which was enhanced by the reflection of the light.

I feel that I have communicated my interest toward her without the need to talk for exactly ten months now. I started seeing her in a special way since November of 2005 right before Thanksgiving.

Aside having everything a woman would like to have when one looks at Anna, she is also very smart, and she seems very secure of herself. Anna's major at school is Literature. This week she showed an interest in reading *A Visitor Awaits You*, my book. Three weeks prior I told Anna I wanted to find a collaborator/editor for the book. What is left for me to see is what Anna's reaction is going to be after she reads the book.

My Physical Health

Since March of 2006 I have been undergoing through lots of medical tests because I have had lower abdominal pain for about a year now. The doctors are doing what is called a 'rule out diagnosis process' and will stop performing medical tests until they find what is wrong, that is if there is something wrong with me. A urologist started performing Medical Tests on me since March of this year. He performed an ultrasound of my kidneys, a cystoscopy and a biopsy procedure and everything that has to do with my kidneys or bladder is fine. A month ago, a gastroenterologist performed a colonoscopy on me and last week a gynecologist performed a dilatation and curettage. I am concerned about this whole thing and I have been working myself out psychologically. It seems my physical health is giving up on me when for the first time in six years I feel ready and want to live life without a doubt. I am also looking into the possibility of getting my own place soon.

I am finally at peace because last Tuesday I was told that I had no cancer. The experience I went through for the last six months waiting for answers for each medical test they performed on me is a good one. I was able to see the value of life though my words of comfort while undergoing all the medical tests was "I always wanted to die anyways."

Back to Anna

My interest in Anna went away, actually she sent it away. One thing I know is that she knew how much I liked her. After this I lost interest in going to the Gay and Lesbian groups, even though I was able to socialize with the group for the whole summer season. Little by little I began not to fit in. The more they knew about me the more they seemed to distance themselves, especially the girls I tried dating.

The Things Which I Did Not Plan

It has been tremendously difficult for me to understand and tolerate the things which I did not plan but which came into my life. I never thought I would constantly have problems at work to eventually have to leave my job as an Auditor. I almost lost my sister Tamara. I had to let my Ricky go. It was never in my plans to live at a Board and Care for the mentally ill.

And to think that I always thought I would kill myself; if I ever lost my job, if I ever lost Tamara, if I ever lost Ricky. The help that I have gotten from my psychiatrist and from my psychotherapist which started in the year of 2004 is what has kept me here.

And Apart I Went

So, I closed my eyes as the tears ran, and apart I went to a distant land, where I found myself laying on the grass as the night came in as the night went out until these, my tears, were frozen by the caressing of the morning breeze. My way of telling you that my life was on hold for quite some time, I guess for years honestly there are great periods of time in which I do not know what I did. I was away from the friends I once had, I was away from my family, I was just passing the days, I was just being and no more. Perhaps I was doing the best with what I had which was nothing. I guess I lived in the nothing, in that dark place I imagined as being the nothing when I challenged the nuns back in school when I was little.

Tamara Moved Out
of California

My sister Tamara went to Florida after the last major surgery. She wanted to start a new life. She wanted to leave her husband. I did not hear much of Tamara while she was away. Our friendship had ended abruptly, I never knew why, I do recall asking my mother why, but I never had answers. It is as if I was on the way between Tamara and someone who did not want the best for Tamara. I could not be there for her anymore. I only know that I missed my sister a great deal.

Yicky

During the year of 2008 I needed company and I felt emotionally ready to get another pet back in my life. I asked my brother Alfredo to go with me to the pet shelter so that I could adopt a pet. I approached a cage where there were about six dogs in it and the first dog to approach me happened to be a female Chihuahua, right there and then I knew this was the one I wanted to have. I filed the paperwork and I was able to take this dog with me on the same day we went to the shelter. I named her Yicky, in honor to my previous Chihuahua whose name was Ricky, I just replaced the R with a Y, to name it almost the same as Ricky. This female Chihuahua has been very good to me, we go for long walks every day, she is a very exciting and happy dog.

My Mother Almost Left Us

In November of the year 2013 my mother was told that she had to see a cardiologist. She did not tell anyone, and she planned her New Year's trip to Las Vegas as she used to every year. About six months later and in the year of 2014, she underwent major surgery. Once again same as with what I did for Tamara, I was by my mother's side every single day. I would sleep with her in the hospital, making sure that the best of doctors and the best of hospitals were chosen for her medical care. My mother made it through, she survived. During this time Tamara was back in California, first she would be here visiting and eventually she moved back to California.

Dee-Dee

I took my niece Michelle to the pet shelter because she has never been to one. While there we saw a very tiny female Chihuahua, we approached her and played with her and when we turned around in order to leave this tiny dog started crying. Michelle and I looked at each other and we felt very sorry for the dog and I ended up adopting it. So, my family grew bigger, now it is Yicky, Dee-Dee and me.

I Moved to the Desert

During the year of 2018 I moved to Cathedral City, I am right on the border of Palm Springs and Cathedral City. Population in this city is less than 50,000. During Summer the temperature is as high as 120 degrees. It is very nice and quiet to live in the desert. The sky is always clear you can see the stars at night. We have days when it is very windy, out of nothing we get sandstorms. I always wanted to live in a small and quiet place and I guess I found the place now.

Tamara No More

I recall I was once communicating with my supervisor Elena from work. It was about my sister Tamara and her struggles and fight to remain with us after her suicide attempt in 1998. During this conversation I wrote: And if my sister ever dies my tomorrow will be my yesterday and my yesterday today. I think I meant to say that I would not acknowledge time after the moment my sister would die. Well, that day finally came. I did not lose my sister back in the year of 1998. We made it through over and over again from all of the ups and down in her recovery throughout the years. One evening during the year of 2018 I fell asleep on the living room sofa. I had a rough night I know I moved a great deal while sleeping and I know I had tremendous heat in my body putting my blanket aside many times. I guess I was struggling in my sleep with something. The following morning at around 7:30 am I received a phone call from Aunt Marcia. She asked me if I was sitting down and then she informed me that someone in the family died. I asked her if it was my mother, she said no then I asked if it was my mother's sister she said no, then she went ahead and told me that Tamara had died. They found her at 3:00 am dead in the bathroom. Tamara did not die inside the bathroom on the night of her suicide attempt in 1998.

Tamara died almost 20 years later in the bathroom. On the night Tamara died her ex-husband was in the bedroom. He was sleeping. It is very difficult for me to think Tamara is no longer with us, when I remember that indeed she is no longer with us I immediately erase that thought from my mind. I remember one time in front of my mother, Tamara and I had a conversation and we told each other that if she died before I did, she would send signals to me and vice versa. Well, a week ago I was cleaning my place and when I got to the living room table, I saw Tamara's picture and I spoke to her and told her: "Well Tamara? Where are you? How are you? Do you remember what we told each other that day that whoever would die first would send signals?" I went out that day, when I came back, I noticed things were not in their usual place. The first thing I did was to check all doors and windows to see if anyone had come into my place while I was gone. Everything was very secured and locked up. I proceeded and went inside my bedroom, and turned toward a corner in my bedroom where I have books that belonged to Tamara, these books were kind of not in place. I noticed there was one book that had a card sticking out from one of the books, when I saw it, I pulled the card which is a religious card and it reads: "If you knew how much I love you you'd cry of joy." And just as the card says I did cry and at that moment I knew that Tamara did send me a signal, she was here I felt honored by her visit. Tamara, I love you dearly wherever you are, I am working on 'The Dragonflies in My Mind' as I said I would do. Ever since I started writing this book whenever Tamara saw anything that had a dragonfly on it, she would buy it for me. I have bracelets, a ring, hanging ornaments and other things with dragonflies on it.

A Triumph

I feel that I have won my battle against depression; that queen of darkness who wears a disguise during the day and travels freely at night, offering solutions to those in suffering. I guess there is no need for me to elaborate about this, or is there? I am still here.

The only good thing about the day I cease existing will be that I will be in peace. No longer will there be a need for me to close my eyes to see **The Dragonflies in My Mind.**